POLICE

DRONES AND LAW ENFORCEMENT

LAURA LA BELLA

ROSEN
PUBLISHING

New York

Published in 2017 by The Rosen Publishing Group
29 East 21st Street, New York, NY 10010

Library of Congress Cataloging-in-Publication Data

Names: La Bella, Laura.
Title: Drones and law enforcement / Laura La Bella.
Description: New York : Rosen Publishing, 2017. | Series: Inside the world of
drones | Includes bibliographical references index.
Identifiers: ISBN 9781508173434 (library bound)
Subjects: LCSH: Drone aircraft—Juvenile literature.
Classification: LCC UG1242.D7 L33 2017| DDC 623.74'69—dc23

Manufactured in China

CONTENTS

R odney Brossart is the first American to be arrested with the help of a drone. Brossart, a North Dakota cattle rancher, was sentenced in 2011 to three years in prison for terrorizing police officers. The incident began when six cattle from a neighboring ranch wandered onto Brossart's property. Brossart refused to return the livestock to their rightful owner. When police arrived, he chased them off at gunpoint. A sixteen-hour standoff between Brossart and his three sons and local law enforcement ensued. A SWAT (special weapons and tactics) team came, too. Using a Predator drone loaned from the Department of Homeland Security, the SWAT team was able to locate Brossart and his sons. The drone also provided vital tactical information on when it was safe for officers to enter the premises to make an arrest.

The incident marks the first time a law enforcement agency used drones to directly assist in arresting an American. It's an example of how drones can be useful in law enforcement.

Drones were first developed for military use, initially for target practice and reconnaissance. As technology improved, their use became essential for militaries worldwide. Drones are currently used by the US military for surveillance, reconnaissance, imaging, and air strikes.

As drones' capabilities have expanded, law enforcement agencies have adopted drones as assets. Drones can now be equipped with a range of tools, including color and

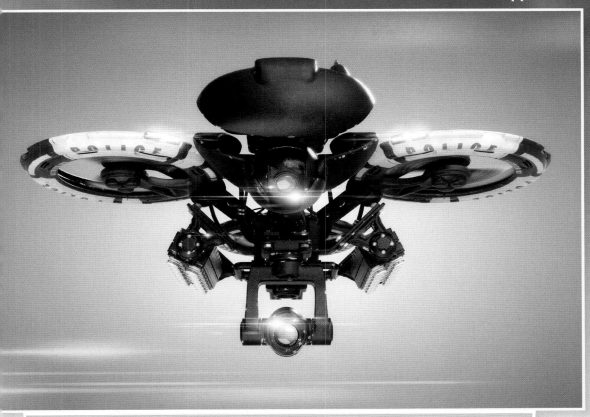

THIS COMPUTER GRAPHIC CONCEPTUAL RENDERING ILLUSTRATES WHAT A COMMON LAW ENFORCEMENT DRONE MIGHT LOOK LIKE IN THE NEAR FUTURE.

black-and-white cameras, facial recognition software, image intensifiers, radar, sensors, infrared imaging, extremely sensitive microphones capable of monitoring conversations, and weaponry. Law enforcement agencies are beginning to explore the use of drones in traffic enforcement, narcotics interdiction, security, terrorism/counterterrorism-related security/surveillance, and more.

The use of these high-tech "eyes in the sky" is not without controversy. Currently, there are few guidelines or laws for regulating drone use by law enforcement. The US Constitution's Fourth Amendment protects citizens against illegal search and seizure and requires a search warrant for law enforcement to search your home, your person, or your personal effects, but only when sufficient evidence strongly indicates a crime has been committed. Drones, with their ability to search property and conduct surveillance, have the potential to produce evidence of a visible crime—whether they are tasked to look for one or not. Drones deployed without regulations and oversight, and without regard to privacy rights, could present an unprecedented compromise of civil liberties.

Did the use of the Predator drone violate Brossart's right to privacy even though a search warrant was issued to law enforcement? Is there a legal distinction between a search conducted by humans, who are limited in their abilities to see evidence when the search is conducted on foot or via helicopter, and a drone, which has state-of-the art optic technology that enables the device to conduct a search in immense detail? These questions and more are at the center of ongoing conversations about how drones can and should be used to aid law enforcement in their day-to-day activities.

CHAPTER 1

THE EVOLUTION OF DRONES AND DRONE TECHNOLOGY

I n North Dakota, a prisoner transport bus stopped at a rest stop in a rural area near the city of Fargo, in January 2011, according to the *Grand Forks Herald*. One of the prisoners escaped from the van and ran into a nearby cornfield. At the time, law enforcement officers in North Dakota did not have access to drone technology.

With one at their disposal, a twenty-two-hour search for the suspect could possibly have been chopped down to half the time, or maybe only two or three hours. A drone hovering overhead and searching the cornfields would have been able to cover an exponentially greater amount of ground than search parties on foot. It would also render moot calling out helicopters or other personnel- and resource-intensive search tools.

WHAT IS A DRONE?

A drone is an unmanned aircraft. It can be as small as a hand-held, remote-controlled airplane, as large as a spy plane, or any size in between. Often referred to as UAVs (unmanned aerial vehicles) or RPAS (remotely piloted aerial systems), drones are operated in one of two ways. On-board computers are programmed to carry out specific flight paths and tasks, such as surveillance. Drones can also be operated by trained crewmembers stationed on the ground. These crewmembers control the flight of the aircraft, analyze the images or information being collected, and, if appropriate,

In March 2015, members of a French police intervention unit scale a building as a drone surveils a hostage situation inside, where a father was threatening his children's safety.

take further action. In the case of military drones, this might include deciding whether to fire upon a target.

Drones are often used in situations where a flight piloted by a person is too risky, too difficult, or simply impossible. Drones have been used to fly into hostile airspace for reconnaissance, drop flotation devices to stranded people in a flood, survey a waterfront for sharks, and conduct searches for missing people in areas that are not easily accessible. Many drones can stay in flight for up to eighteen hours and can report information back to controllers in real time.

HOW DO DRONES WORK?

Drones are intelligent pieces of technology. They differ from remote-controlled airplanes and helicopters in that many aspects of their operation are autonomous, or independent, from their operator. With remote-controlled airplanes or helicopters, the operator is engaged in every part of the flying process. The airplane or helicopter cannot do anything without the operator instructing it to via a remote control.

Drones differ in that they can hover, fly, stay in a specific position in the sky, or navigate their surroundings without the aid of a pilot or crewmember at the controls. These are tasks a remote-controlled airplane or helicopter cannot do.

A basic drone is made with a sturdy frame that can withstand the pressures of flying in low-altitude airspace. They can have propellers or wings, depending on their design, which create the lift they need to become airborne, and a motor and battery that make the device operational and provide power. Drones are outfitted with flight-controller boards. These tiny computers have special sensors for measuring movement, rotation, and gravity, enabling the drone to fly and maintain its position in the air. Drones can be outfitted with special equipment—from cameras and sensors to ammunition and missiles—depending on their use.

Unlike remote-controlled airplanes and helicopters, a drone's controller can be stationed around the world. While drones take off and land local to the area in which they are being used, crewmembers can be monitoring and assisting in the drone's flight from anywhere. For example, drones being used by the US military in Afghanistan are controlled by crewmembers located seven thousand miles (11,265 kilometers) away on a US military base in Nevada.

Another key difference between a drone and a remote-controlled airplane or helicopter is the involvement of the Federal Aviation Administration (FAA). Hobbyists can fly model airplanes and helicopters without restrictions, but it is illegal to operate a drone as a civilian above four hundred feet (122 meters). Drones may not be operated beyond the line of sight, a term used to describe an unobstructed view of the device by its operator, nor can they be used for any commercial reason unless the drone and its operator receive permission from the FAA.

The FAA issues certificates of authorization to public entities, such as NASA, the National Oceanic and Atmospheric Administration (NOAA), and other federal agencies, police departments, and universities.

FROM MILITARY TO LAW ENFORCEMENT

While the drones being used today are complex pieces of intelligent machinery, they are not a new twenty-first century innovation. Drones of a sort, albeit far more primitive in their use and design, date back to the early 1900s, when the US military used them for target practice. More modern drones were developed for use in World War I and World War II, but even those were little more than remote-controlled airplanes. It was in the years preceding and including the Vietnam War, in the 1950s and into the '60s and '70s, when drones were used in more strategic ways as the technology improved and better, more efficient drones were designed.

It wasn't until after the September 11, 2001, terrorist attacks when the

THIS MQ-9 REAPER UAV, SHOWN AT A HIGH ALTITUDE, IS THE PRIMARY DRONE USED BY THE US MILITARY FOR STRIKES AGAINST ENEMY FORCES.

TYPES OF DRONES BY SIZE AND CAPABILITY

Drones are made in a range of sizes and with capabilities that enable them to accomplish specific types of missions. There is no set standard of classification for drones, so most are categorized by size:

- *Very Small Drones*: These drones, also called microdrones or nanodrones, can measure as small as an insect. They are normally no larger than 20 inches (51 centimeters) long. These drones are used primarily for spying. They can maneuver into small places to gather intelligence information. Future versions are planned that might even be invisible to the naked eye.
- *Small Drones*: These drones measure between 20 inches (51 cm) and 7 feet (2 meters). Because of their smaller size, these drones do not take off and land autonomously. Instead, operators must throw the drones into the air for take off.
- *Medium Drones*: Medium drones can weigh as much as 440 pounds (200 kilograms) and are too large to be carried by a person. These drones also have a wingspan of 16 to 33 feet (5 to 10 m).
- *Large Drones*: Typically the size of a small aircraft, large drones are most often used in combat or when sending people into a situation that is too dangerous or a location that is inaccessible. Large drones are used predominantly by the military.

MILITARY DRONES ARE OPERATED FROM REMOTE CONTROL STATIONS, SUCH AS THIS SECRET ONE IN THE PERSIAN GULF THAT RUNS MISSIONS AGAINST THE MILITANT GROUP ISIS, OR ISLAMIC STATE OF IRAQ AND SYRIA.

The US military classifies drones by their capabilities, too:

- *Very Close-Range Drones*: These drones have a range of 2 to 3 miles (3.2 to 4.8 km) and battery life of 20 to 45 minutes.
- *Close-Range Drones*: With a capacity to fly in a 30-mile (48 km) range, close-range drones have a flight time of one to six hours and conduct surveillance missions.
- *Short-Range Drones*: Short-range drones can fly up to 93 miles (150 km) and have a flight time of eight to twelve hours. These drones are for surveillance and reconnaissance.
- *Mid-Range Drones*: With a capacity for a 450-mile (724 km) range, mid-range drones are high-speed aircraft that

(CONTINUED ON THE NEXT PAGE)

(CONTINUED FROM THE PREVIOUS PAGE)

not only conduct surveillance but can also gather meteo-rological data.

- *Endurance Drones*: Endurance drones can fly for up to thirty-six hours and can reach heights of thirty thousand feet (9,144 m). These drones are used for sophisticated surveillance as well as for combat. The Predator drone, used by the US Air Force, is outfitted with missiles and other ammunition. It can carry out precision strikes on targets.

US military began widespread use of drones. With the US invasions of Afghanistan and the later invasion of Iraq, drones became an essential tool of the US armed forces. Drones were used for surveillance and some were outfitted with missiles that could destroy targets. Modern-day drones now carry still and video cameras, image intensifiers, ammunition, and various instruments that can process real-time data on weather, airborne chemicals, and radioactive materials. Since 2002, the United States has deployed more than eleven thousand military drones on a wide range of missions.

POPULAR USES FOR DRONES

Drones have gained popularity outside of their military uses. They have become a trendy recreational alternative for model airplane hobbyists who want to fly a more complex piece of machinery. They have also been used for civilian (nonmilitary and nonpolice) uses including:

- Commercial aerial surveillance, for monitoring livestock, wildfire mapping, pipeline security, home security, road patrol, and antipiracy
- Professional aerial surveying, including photogrammetry and LiDAR (light detection and ranging)
- Filmmaking, for aerial shots that would otherwise require a helicopter or other manned aircraft, which is more expensive
- Journalism and news gathering, for times when a story is in a dangerous location or when a cameraman cannot gain safe access
- Search and rescue, to aid in searching for missing persons or animals
- Scientific research, for accessing areas where humans cannot go, such as into the eye of a hurricane or a volcano

CHAPTER 2

FIRST RESPONSE

The use of drones by law enforcement agencies is reshaping the way these organizations respond to crimes and other incidents. Ben Miller, a Mesa County, Colorado, sheriff's deputy, spent a year creating his police department's drone program, including comprehensive training for deputies on the force. Miller's drone program is used primarily for crime scene and accident reconstruction. In an interview with Reuters news service, Miller said the department's drone, a DraganflyerX6 quadcopter, can be programmed to fly two concentric circles, at two different elevations, around a crime scene or accident, to reconstruct what occurred. The drone can capture more than seventy photos that are uploaded to a computer. Online digital-mapping software

DRONES CAN ACCESS AREAS THAT PEOPLE CANNOT, SUCH AS ALONG A SKYSCRAPER'S SURFACE. THIS TYPE OF SURVEILLANCE AIDS LAW ENFORCEMENT BY PROVIDING INFORMATION QUICKLY AND SAFELY.

produces a 3D reconstruction of the crime scene or accident for investigators and, later, for a judge and jury at trial.

Miller's department is one of 609 agencies nationwide that are using drones to assist officers with law enforcement, firefighting, border patrol, military training, disaster relief, and search and rescue. The number of agencies that has received permission from the Federal Aviation Administration, which oversees nonmilitary aviation in the United States, to use drones has increased, 423 agencies in 2013 compared with 146 in 2009.

POLICE EMERGENCIES

As the idea of drone use spreads, law enforcement agencies are recognizing all of the areas in which drones can be beneficial. Drones have the capacity to be an extra set of eyes and ears in situations that are either inaccessible to humans or are deemed too dangerous for officers to go. They are also proving to be valuable tools for reconnaissance and surveillance.

Hostage negotiation: During a hostage situation, a drone has the potential to get closer to the drama and report real-time video and audio from inside a home, bank, or other location where hostages are being held. A drone can help investigators see what's going on inside the building without risking the lives of officers. Drones can be used for reconnaissance, surveillance, and for dropping off medical supplies, food, or other necessities needed by the hostages or their captor.

SPECIAL PERMISSIONS

The Federal Aviation Administration (FAA) regulates national airspace. According to the FAA, the United States has the busiest and most complex airspace in the world, which is why regulation and registration of drones by companies, government agencies (including law enforcement), and individual hobbyists is needed.

Drones do not show up on most radar, which poses a problem for manned aircraft, like airplanes, because if an airplane cannot see a drone on radar, neither pilots nor air traffic controllers are able to take evasive actions.

The FAA has provided special permissions for law enforcement agencies to operate drones for a particular purpose and in a particular area. These permissions, called a COA, which stands for "certificate of waiver or authorization," permit public agencies and organizations to operate a drone or other unmanned aircraft system. COAs are issued for a limited time, usually two years. For law enforcement agencies that apply for and receive a COA, drones can be used as long as they are not operated in highly populated areas and the aircraft is observed to ensure that the drone is operated and controlled in accordance to right-of-way rules in airspace.

Bomb investigation and diffusion: Drones can help provide situational awareness, which in law enforcement means to know what is happening around you. In certain scenarios, such as a bomb threat or bomb investigation, it is necessary to identify, process, and comprehend all of the critical pieces of information about what is happening and when to get a sense of the entire situation. In a bomb investigation, a drone is able to get close to a bomb, survey the area for additional weapons or people, and provide valuable feedback without sending a team of officers into a highly insecure and dangerous environment. A drone can also fly over the bomb and provide bomb technicians with images and information about the device, which can aid in its diffusion.

Missing persons: A child runs off at a crowded amusement park, a hiker becomes lost in the wilderness, an Alzhei-

DRONES OUTFITTED WITH CAMERAS CAN GATHER VIDEO EVIDENCE OR SURVEILLANCE OF A SITUATION, WHICH CAN PROVIDE DETAILED INFORMATION THAT ALLOWS POLICE DEPARTMENTS TO ACT QUICKLY IN EMERGENCIES.

mer's patient wanders from home—people go missing in a wide variety of circumstances. Drones that are equipped with cameras, license-plate readers, and facial recognition software could increase the probability (and speed) of locating missing persons. Drones can also provide real-time intelligence on terrain, weather conditions, and other site information that could become crucial during a search and rescue mission.

Criminal surveillance and pursuit: Drones armed with facial recognition software are capable of identifying criminals during surveillance. The software is programmed to review and compare people's faces in a crowd with faces stored in a database. If a match occurs, the drone can alert law enforcement that a suspect or criminal is in the vicinity. Drones can also pursue a suspect who is on the run by following the suspect from the air.

Drug interdiction: Drug interdiction is the act of disrupting or delaying the illegal smuggling or transportation of drugs. In February 2016, Dutch police were able to identify and shut down an illegal marijuana-growing site when a drone noticed that one house in a neighborhood had no snow on its roof. The heat lamps used to grow the marijuana were so warm that they heated the air in the attic of the home and it melted the snow on the roof. The drone's operator picked up on the anomaly during routine surveillance and local law enforcement investigated further.

Crime scene analysis: Crime scene investigation is about preserving evidence left behind when a crime has taken place. That evidence can help investigators piece together what happened and assist in helping them identify and arrest

IN LIVERPOOL, UNITED KINGDOM, OFFICERS USE DRONES TO VISUALLY ANTICIPATE POTENTIAL PROBLEMS DURING "MAD FRIDAY," A CELEBRATORY DAY THAT OFTEN CAUSES CROWD-CONTROL CONCERNS.

a suspect. Keeping evidence clean, or undisturbed, is essential to making sure a crime scene is not contaminated. A drone can help in this scenario. Normally a crime scene investigator and other law enforcement personnel are on the scene and document any evidence they find. But they could track dirt and dust into a crime scene from their shoes. They could also unknowingly disturb a key piece of evidence. A drone can photograph a scene, take samples of blood, locate a weapon, and otherwise scan a crime scene.

Active shooter/mass shooting scenarios: In a scenario in which an active shooter is aiming a loaded weapon at innocent people and killing them, it can be difficult for law enforcement officers to find a way to get close enough to the suspect to stop the shooting and apprehend him or her. An armed drone can enter an active shooter situation and shoot or kill a suspect to end the violence.

CHAPTER 3

CRIME PREVENTION, SECURITY, AND EMERGENCY MANAGEMENT

In 2013, the United Nations launched its first unarmed surveillance drones, according to *Wired* magazine. The drones were tasked with flying over two countries, the Democratic Republic of Congo and Rwanda, as part of a UN peacekeeping mission. The two countries have been embroiled in violent conflicts between their governments and various armed civilian groups.

The UN deployed the drones not only for surveillance but also as a visual deterrent to remind hostile groups that they are being watched. Drones, and their sophisticated capabilities, are being utilized in many capacities to help aid in crime prevention, crime deterrence, security, and emergency/disaster response.

BORDER PATROL

At Grand Forks Air Force Base in northeastern North Dakota, crewmembers operate nine Predator drones for US Customs and Border Protection. This government agency is responsible for protecting the nation's borders and preventing the illegal entry of people and goods. It also protects and ensures the trading of goods and services between the United States and other nations. Crewmembers fly drones along the US-Mexican border and the US-Canadian border looking for any signs of illegal border crossings.

A large Predator drone carries high-tech radar that can track people or vehicles over a wide area. The Predator's radar is so precise that it can detect footprints and tire tracks. The drone can also tell crewmembers the direction in which people or vehicles are moving. Crewmembers assess this data and inform border patrol agents on the ground, who can conduct a more thorough investigation and, when necessary, apprehend illegal immigrants or confiscate illegal goods.

The US-Mexican border stretches more than two thousand miles (3,219 km), from Texas to California, and is very diverse in its terrain. In addition to legal points of entry, such as ports and border crossings, there are stretches of barren desert, mountainous terrain, and a portion of the Rio Grande, all of which are accessible to those looking to enter or transport goods into the United States illegally. In some sections, an old fence is the only thing separating the two countries. It would be impossible to monitor every inch of the border on a continuous

THE US DEPARTMENT OF HOMELAND SECURITY, WHICH OVERSEES US CUSTOMS AND BORDER PROTECTION, FLIES DRONES ALONG THE BORDER BETWEEN THE UNITED STATES AND MEXICO.

basis, which is why the US Customs and Border Protection's drone program is a necessity.

In 2013, Predator drones monitoring US borders were directly responsible for providing information that led to the seizure of $341 million of contraband by border patrol agents. The contraband included drugs, money, and weapons. Border security has been a significant part of US homeland security efforts. Drones provide a way to assist in monitoring and preventing drug cartels, traffickers, and terrorists from exploiting holes in the current border control and security system.

COUNTERTERRORISM AND COUNTERINSURGENCY

Counterterrorism encompasses all of the activities—spying, surveillance, reconnaissance, interrogation, force, and more—that are used by the US government to prevent, deter, preempt, and/or respond to terrorism and terrorist activities. Counterinsurgency includes similar activities to those used in counterterrorism, except these actions are aimed at groups that have a political goal. Insurgents want to overthrow a government, take control of specific portions of land or resources, or further their political motives in violent ways. Drones are one tactic in the government's arsenal of ways to thwart terrorism and insurgency.

Drones were used by the US military before the 9/11 terrorist attacks. After the attacks, drone use became a significant tactic of warfare in American military and counterterrorism efforts. Drones have a number of advantages: they reduce risk to military personnel; they do not require a large military presence; and they can be armed with missiles to target specific individuals, vehicles, or buildings. One of the most significant advantages of drones is their combination of intelligence-gathering capabilities and their capacity to use force. Crewmembers controlling drones are able to monitor real-time feedback, report what they see to a military commander, and take immediate action if ordered to do so.

DRONES AND THE RULES OF THE ROAD

Traffic laws are notorious for being inconsistently enforced. If a police officer isn't watching the particular stretch of road you are driving on and you happen to be speeding, you are breaking a law but you will not be held accountable for it. Yet, if a traffic stop is set up and police are checking your car's registration and yours is expired, you'll receive a ticket for the infraction.

Drones used to observe traffic and monitor roadways for traffic violations can help enforce existing traffic laws,

THIS DRONE IMAGE OF A TRAFFIC CIRCLE IN REYKJAVIK, ICELAND, IS ONE EXAMPLE OF THE KIND OF IMAGES THAT CAN HELP MUNICIPALITIES ADDRESS ROAD CONGESTION WITH REAL-TIME INFORMATION.

PLATESMART: A SLIPPERY SLOPE FOR PRIVACY?

PlateSmart Technologies has developed license plate identification software that can be installed on drones. This software will enable law enforcement officers to identify plate numbers, which can tell officers who the vehicle is registered to, personal information about the owner, such as their driving record, criminal record and address, and the vehicle's state or country of origin. The software can also be used to identify potential criminals or those driving with a suspended license.

While there are reasonable uses for the scanning and collection of license plate data, among them national security, privacy concerns are arising about whether this type of data collection is a violation of individual civil liberties.

The collection of license plate numbers is already happening on a daily basis throughout the Unites States. Small cameras, called automated license plate readers, have been installed all over the country. Each day, thousands of images are uploaded to national databases that collect information on the car itself, its exact location, and the time and date it was there. Police departments throughout the nation access these databases when they are trying to identify vehicles that were involved in a crime.

Currently, there is no law that prevents public agencies from sharing and/or selling the license plate numbers. With drones, which can be deployed to follow a suspect who is driving in a car, this data collection and its use are coming under more scrutiny. There is great skepticism nowadays about whether proper protocols will be taken to ensure that the privacy of citizens—and that of the society at large—is protected.

which can keep people safer and potentially cut down on the number of traffic accidents. In highly populated areas, where traffic can be heavy, drones can monitor traffic patterns, report on delays that can impact the movement of traffic, and identify problem areas that need to be addressed.

DRONES AND SECURITY

With drones being used widely by military and law enforcement agencies, it's just a matter of time before drones are implemented for use in private or corporate security. Since 2012, when a Japanese company announced the creation of the world's first drone for private security, dozens of other security companies have introduced drones as well. While regulations are still being determined for commercial drone use in the United States, other countries have begun to implement drones in a wide range of security applications.

The city of Abu Dhabi, the capital of the United Arab Emirates, is using drones to assess and monitor accidents and to provide information during search and rescue operations. The city is also using drones to monitor the Port of Abu Dhabi, where cruise ships, cargo vessels, and other shipments arrive and depart each day. Gatwick Airport, located outside London, England, is among the first airports in the world to use drones for on-site safety.

Officials running the 2014 Winter Olympics in Sochi and the 2014 World Cup in Brazil both utilized drones to provide twenty-four-hour surveillance over high-traffic areas, to

THIS OFFICER PREPARES TO LAUNCH A DRONE FOR A POLICE DRILL IN PREPARATION FOR THE 2016 TOKYO MARATHON. DRONES ARE ABLE TO MONITOR LARGE CROWDS FOR POTENTIAL TROUBLE.

track and monitor crowds, and to report any incidents to law enforcement on the ground.

At the 2014 South by Southwest festival, a film, interactive media, and music festival and conference in Austin, Texas, Chaotic Moon Studios demonstrated a personal security drone. The drone, which was equipped with a stun gun, can disable an intruder once an alarm has been triggered at a private residence or business. Unfortunately, its test shocked a company intern. While he was unharmed, it prompted Austin police to uphold a citywide drone ban the following year at the event.

CHAPTER 4

PROTECTING THE NATURAL WORLD

The latest in drone technology is offering environmental groups an innovative way to ensure that governments, corporations, and others are in compliance with environmental and conservation laws. Drones are also assisting in conservation efforts to protect the environment as well as the planet's natural resources. Drone technology promises better protection of the environment and government accountability for its action or inaction.

Environmental protection agencies, agencies that monitor national parks, and nonprofit wildlife protection organizations may often be underfunded and understaffed. Drones are emerging as a low-cost, highly efficient way for these groups to curb illegal fishing and poaching, decrease and eliminate illegal exploitation of private or public lands, oversee logging practices, monitor proper waste disposal, and even track and monitor animals that are on the endangered species list.

WHAT IS ENVIRONMENTAL LAW?

AN OCTOCOPTER HOVERS IN YASUNI NATIONAL PARK, PART OF THE AMAZON JUNGLE IN ECUADOR. ITS MISSION IS TO STUDY THE VEGETATION AND LIFE OF THE CANOPY OF THIS ENVIRONMENT.

Environmental laws can address the effects of human activity on the natural environment. There are laws in place to regulate and monitor pollution, specifically the quality of the air and water; waste management, including the transport, treatment, storage, and disposal of all waste; the removal of contaminants that have seeped into water and soil; management of natural resources, such as forests and timber harvesting; preservation and control of fishing, game, and other wildlife; and sustainable development, which ensures that future generations can meet their needs through managed environmental regulation.

Environmental laws are important because they serve to protect natural resources, such as land, air, water, and soil. Many natural resources, such as coal and oil, are not renewable. The strict management of these resources can ensure that future generations will have access to these resources for their survival. Enforcing these laws can be difficult and collecting evidence that laws have been broken and by whom is a challenge. Drones have begun to play a significant role in monitoring the environment and enforcing a wide range of environmental laws.

AN OPERATOR CONTROLS A DRONE IN HOPES OF CAPTURING SHARK FOOTAGE FOR ONE OF THE DISCOVERY CHANNEL'S "SHARK WEEK" SPECIALS.

Detection and detention of illegal poachers/protection for endangered species: The World Wildlife Fund, which received financial support from Google, will begin to implement drones as part of a remote aerial survey system that will serve to detect and detain illegal poachers. Drones that catch illegal fishing and poaching activities can record these activities via onboard video cameras. These videos can be presented as evidence in a court of law, where a recorded stream of video can show evidence of a violation.

In parts of Africa, endangered elephants live on isolated preserves dedicated to their survival. These preserves are underfunded by their local and national governments and consistently at risk for being intruded upon by poachers looking to sell the animals to illegal traders or kill them for their valuable tusks. The Tanzania National Parks Authority, with support from the Tanzanian army, is now using drones to monitor who enters the park. The park can watch its grounds around the clock to catch poachers. Nongovernmental agencies (NGOs), which do not have the authority to apprehend poachers, can direct their drones to track poachers back to traders who buy endangered animals. NGOs can help direct local law enforcement to the location of such criminals.

Protection for conservation researchers: Conservation researchers examine the environment to assess the overall quality of forests, parks, rangelands, wildlife and other natural resources. They work throughout the world to better understand how changes to the environment affect local conditions as well as how changes may affect the larger

DRONES HELP FARMERS KEEP A CLOSE EYE ON CROPS

When your vegetable farm covers hundreds of acres, having an eye on your crops can be difficult. Drones are providing farmers with unprecedented opportunities to monitor their agriculture with accurate, high-resolution images of their fields. Farmers, who fly their drones within 120 meters (394 ft) of the ground, well under the 400-meter (1,312 ft) limit the FAA has put in place, can see things they cannot when they inspect their plants up close.

With these top-down views of their fields, farmers can visually inspect the entire crop, including crops in the middle of fields that are harder to access; spot water shortages in soil or early signs of drought; manage water and irrigation schedules to maintain proper soil moisture; assess crop health, including the identification of pests and any damage they have created; monitor soil health and soil erosion; and determine crop maturity, allowing them to establish peak times for harvesting.

Data from an infrared camera on a drone can also spot differences between healthy and distressed plants, allowing farmers to address issues early so they can harvest more healthy plants, which results in better profits for their farm. Drones can help farmers use their resources more efficiently and even solve problems affecting their crops in a more timely manner.

environmental ecosystem as a whole. Drones have become a useful tool in conservation research. They allow conservationists to monitor, photograph, and study areas of the world that are inaccessible to humans. They also provide protection and safety. Poachers in conflict zones are often armed, presenting a risk to researchers hoping to better understand the environment in these parts of the world. Drones allow researchers to continue to conduct research without having to come in contact with dangerous individuals.

Drones also allow researchers to conduct an initial review of an area at a lower cost to see if it's a location worth examining further. Some locations are difficult to

THIS DRONE—A SPREADING WINGS S900 MODEL—HUMS THROUGH THE AIR DURING THE 2014 UAS MAPPING SYMPOSIUM AND CONFERENCE, AN EVENT CENTERING ON THE MAPPING TECHNOLOGIES OF UNMANNED VEHICLES.

get to, and without knowing for sure what they will find, it's expensive to send a team of researchers with food, supplies, and expensive equipment. Drones can provide an overview of the landscape through high-resolution photographs that can help researchers determine if an area is worth investing time and money to conduct a full on-site analysis.

Environmental data collection: Drones are making it easier than ever to collect data on the environment. From mapping coastal erosion, receding glaciers, and diminishing ocean water levels to assessing the physical conditions of rivers and the movement of different migratory animals, drones are making it possible to collect more and more information about the environment. With sophisticated imaging systems, drones can aid researchers in collecting data more efficiently and more affordably.

Compliance with environmental laws: Environmental groups see the use of drones as a tool to help them monitor loggers, farmers, and corporations to make sure these entities are staying compliant with industry standards and environmental law. Similar to how dashboard cameras in police cars can capture traffic stops and the actions of both suspects and officers, drones can collect evidence of wrongdoing and violations of environmental law. Drones enable governments, NGOs, corporations, and interest groups to oversee activity in an efficient and affordable way.

CHAPTER 5

The Changing Legal Horizon

With all their documented benefits and potential for good, drone use by law enforcement is not without controversy. Privacy advocates are insisting that the US government regulate the use of drones with clear-cut guidelines on what they can and cannot be used for, along with punishments for violations.

In 2012, the International Association of Chiefs of Police published a list of recommended guidelines for how and when agencies can use drones in law enforcement scenarios. The list, supported by the American Civil Liberties Union, included the following:

- Police should not be able to keep images taken by drones unless they are relevant to a crime.

- Police should provide the public with warnings or announcements of when drones will be used.
- Drone use by law enforcement should be accountable, with their operation being tracked and audited on a regular basis.
- Police should not be able to outfit drones with any kind of weapons.

PRIVACY AND THE FOURTH AMENDMENT

The primary concern surrounding drone use is the potential for violations to the US Constitution's Fourth Amendment. The Fourth Amendment protects you from illegal search and seizure, which means law enforcement agencies cannot search your home, person, or personal effects unless sufficient evidence strongly indicates wrongdoing. Even with sufficient evidence, a search warrant

AT THE MILIPOL INTERNATIONAL TRADE FAIR FOR SECURITY IN FRANCE, DRONES ARE A CENTRAL ATTRACTION. THEY ARE BECOMING SOUGHT OUT BY LAW ENFORCEMENT AGENCIES.

must be issued by a judge before a search can begin. This amendment has been a cornerstone of privacy from government intrusion since 1791, when the amendment was added to the Constitution. In the simplest of terms, the Fourth Amendment makes it impossible for law enforcement to enter your home, search you physically, or examine your personal belongings without due cause and without a search warrant issued by a judge.

The issue with drones comes with their ability to conduct surveillance, which is the close observation of people or activities. With drones, the ability to search property or conduct surveillance of individuals has become easier and, in some instances, has produced evidence of a visible crime by accident. In the court case *California v. Ciraolo*, police officers identified marijuana plants in a suspect's backyard from a plane at an altitude of one thousand feet (305 m) after a tip had been called in about the suspect and his property. A search warrant was later obtained and law enforcement officers raided the property. The suspect pleaded guilty to growing marijuana.

Later, a California Court of Appeal reversed the charge on the grounds that the initial search, conducted by a plane, was not done with a search warrant, which violated the suspect's right to privacy. The case made its way to the Supreme Court, which upheld the original conviction. In their decision, the Supreme Court said that the suspect had an unreasonable expectation of privacy. The suspect may have hidden the marijuana from the street, where people walking by could not see it, but the suspect cannot expect privacy in

CHINESE POLICE OFFICERS IN BEIJING PREPARE A DRONE AND ITS CONTROL STATION IN A VAN AS THEY GET READY FOR A MONTH-LONG SURVEILLANCE MISSION TO CATCH OPIUM POPPY GROWERS IN THE ACT.

open airspace, where a law enforcement officer has a public vantage point and has a right to be.

A CHANGING LEGAL LANDSCAPE

A new law, the FAA Reauthorization Act, passed by Congress in February 2012, opens national airspace to drones for commercial, scientific, and law-enforcement use. US president Barack Obama, who has been a strong supporter of military drone use, signed the bill into law. It required the FAA to have regulations in place for drones by 2015 that include a system for licensing drones. As of December 21, 2015, all owners of drones must register their drones with the FAA. Each drone will be marked with a unique number that enables authorities to track down its owner if the drone flies too close to an airport, flies into commercial airspace used by airplanes, or collides with another aircraft. For the FAA, air safety is their main priority, not privacy.

To address privacy concerns, the Drone Aircraft Privacy and Transparency Act of 2015 was created. This act enables the US secretary of transportation to study the use of drones and identify any potential threats they may pose to individual privacy. If drones are integrated into the national airspace and are allowed to fly in the same sky as planes and helicopters, safety and privacy protections will need to be in place. Increasingly, drones are intruding on airspace that has been designated for commercial flights by airlines. Drones pose a significant safety concern since they do not show up on radar used by airplanes.

Some individual states have already passed laws to regulate drone use by their local or state law enforcement agencies. Some states have even prohibited individual drone use. According to the Association for Unmanned Vehicle Systems International (AUVSI), at least six states—Florida, Minnesota, Nevada, North Dakota, Oregon, and Virginia—have passed legislation restricting the commercial use of drones. Another eight have restrictive legislation pending.

DURING A TRAINING EXERCISE IN A MALL IN PARIS, FRANCE, A MEMBER OF AN ELITE FRENCH ANTI-GANG AND COUNTERTERRORISM SQUAD PREPARES TO TEST A DRONE.

THE STATE OF DRONE REGULATION

Some states are not waiting for federal guidelines to be drafted. Instead, they have passed laws that prohibit drone use in numerous scenarios.

California, home to prying paparazzi who stalk celebrities, passed a law that prohibits sending a drone into the airspace above a person's land to capture images or video of that person engaged in private, personal, or family activities without that person's permission. The legislation was crafted in response to the use of drones by paparazzi, who make money by selling images of celebrities to media outlets.

Virginia now requires all law enforcement agencies to obtain a warrant before using a drone for any purpose, except in limited circumstances, which include emergency situations or training exercises related to improving responses to emergency situations.

Other states have established laws prohibiting the use of drones to survey, record, or gather information about critical state infrastructure, such as bridges, power plants, electrical grids, or security.

A CONTROVERSIAL TOPIC

The use of drones has led to a lot of public opposition. Activists want drone use curtailed, sometimes even banned completely. They feel drones further the militarization of local police departments, giving them an unprecedented amount of power and technology to collect information on people's everyday lives.

Privacy concerns beyond the violation of the Fourth Amendment have some people worried that an individual who owns a drone can position it to hover outside the windows of a private home, capturing video, audio, or photographs of people inside. Others are concerned over sharing resources.

Taxpayers whose money goes to appropriating drones (some of which may be quite expensive) and the bureaucrats in charge of them, may be wary of sharing them with other jurisdictions, especially during times when many municipalities are tightening their budgets and otherwise cutting services. In fact, many people who oppose drones consider even moderately priced ones an unnecessary expense that takes away from other local human needs.

CHAPTER 6

FUTURE DRONES

While today's drones may seem advanced now, the plans on the horizon, which will utilize the latest in technology and imaging, make drone development both ambitious and very exciting. As technology continues to progress, drones will become more and more advanced. And, with sales of drones expected to increase significantly—the Federal Aviation Administration estimates that drone purchases could grow from 1.9 million in 2016 to as many as 4.3 million by 2020—people will have access to drones that can do more.

DRONES OUTPACE REGULATION

The FAA has prohibited widespread commercial use of drones, even though drone development is rapid and new innovations are being launched on a regular basis. The demand for drones is immense. Everyone, from private hobbyists to commercial and government entities, wants to use them for a wide range of applications. Due to this demand, the US Congress has instructed the FAA to draft rules for drone use, but they are struggling with how to best regulate an industry that is very young and very quick to evolve. In an interview with PBS, Michael Huerta, an administrator with the FAA, said that ensuring safety is the FAA's primary concern when it comes to drones. "A bedrock principle of aviation is see and avoid," he said in the interview. "And if you don't have a pilot on board the aircraft, you need something that will substitute for that, which will sense other aircraft."

A DRONE ENTHUSIAST PILOTS A UAV NEAR A BRIDGE IN SYDNEY HARBOUR IN SYDNEY, AUSTRALIA. LAW ENFORCEMENT OFFICIALS REMAIN WARY OF DRONES NEAR LANDMARKS AND SENSITIVE SITES.

The FAA has defined three categories for drones and unmanned aircraft: public operations, which encompasses uses for law enforcement, firefighting, border patrol, disaster relief, search and rescue, military training, and other government operational missions; civil operations, which includes any use that doesn't fit the public operations definition; and model aircraft, which covers hobby and recreational uses. The FAA has some regulations in place for drone use, but they are highly restrictive and very limiting. The regulations include:

- Drones cannot be used for commercial purposes that produce revenue or profit.
- Drone flight is restricted to line of sight, which means you must always have eyes on your drones without any sort of technical assistance.
- They are restricted in their use of airspace and cannot be flown above four hundred feet (122 m), within five miles (8 km) of an airport, above any government buildings, or in any national parks.

As the drone industry shifts further away from developing UAVs for military uses and more toward drones for civilian use, it's becoming more important than ever that the FAA have regulations in place for controlling where and how high a drone can be flown. The FAA has proposed further regulations on drone use, including limitations on the weight of drones, speeds at which they can fly, limits on when they can be flown (during daylight hours, for example), and minimum weather visibility ranges, among other considerations and parameters.

ADVANCED DRONES FOR WARFARE

Leading this growth in sales is the development of new, exciting drones from manufacturing companies, universities, and government research facilities. The next generation of drones could be as small as a moth or as large as an airplane. Boeing, an aircraft manufacturing company, is developing the Phantom Eye, a hydrogen-fueled drone that has a 150-foot (46 m) wingspan. It was developed for long-term surveillance and reconnaissance. The prototype can fly at sixty-five thousand feet (20,000 m) for up to four days. The Phantom Eye, an experimental aircraft, flew nine test flights. Boeing has another version of the Phantom Eye that can fly for up to ten days.

Future drones will not be limited to what US military and civilian minds can develop. Another pioneer in the field of drone development is the nation of Israel. Its military has a long history with unmanned aircraft and its spy and technology sectors are among world's most elite. Israel is joining forces with the US military to develop tiny drones that look like bugs. Weighing as little as twenty grams (one ounce), the Butterfly is a drone that contains listening devices and tiny video cameras. The operator also wears a helmet that gives him or her a view inside the Butterfly's cockpit. It's a sensory meld between the operator and the drone.

US NAVY: A PIONEER IN DRONE DEVELOPMENT

The U.S. Navy is known for its ambitious drone program. One goal they set for themselves was to land a drone on an aircraft carrier with minimal guidance from a drone operator—an incredibly difficult task. The movement of aircraft carriers on the water makes this especially hard. Aircraft carriers also have the short runways (about 300 feet, 91 m) compared to those of most airports, which average 2,300 feet (701 m) in length. Even manned aircraft are prone to crashing on aircraft carrier decks.

THE US NAVY'S FIRST CATAPULT LAUNCH OF A DRONE FROM AN AIRCRAFT CARRIER TOOK PLACE IN 2013. THE DRONE WAS AN X-47B. THE MILITARY REMAINS AN IMPORTANT PIONEER IN DRONE DEVELOPMENT.

In 2013, the Navy finally tested a drone's ability to land on an aircraft carrier. The X-47B, a drone shaped like a bat, landed successfully on the deck USS *George H.W. Bush*. The successful test opened up new opportunities for military and civilian maritime surveillance, including that performed by law enforcement agencies. It would now be that much easier to provide security to military and commercial craft on the high seas.

Two years later, in April 2015, the X-47B drone set another historic record when it was involved in the first Autonomous Aerial Refueling (AAR) of an unmanned craft. This milestone unlocked even more uses for naval drones and their civilian counterparts.

Drones can be armed with ammunition and missiles, but when the time comes to hit a target, it's a human who makes the final decision to use lethal force by sending a missile hurtling through the air at a target. A new drone, called the Switchblade, is pushing the boundary of autonomous force.

This drone folds up into a backpack and is fired by a soldier on the ground, who uses a laptop to aim it at a target. The Switchblade is a missile and a drone. It physically hits the target like a missile and can be preprogrammed to hit a specific set of coordinates. A human may still select the target, but it's a new development in drone warfare that gets the military closer to an era when a drone will have the capacity to decide who lives and who dies when it's sent on a mission.

EARN A DEGREE IN DRONE SCIENCE OR ENGINEERING

With the global drone manufacturing industry set to hit the $5 billion mark by 2020, the need for skilled professionals who can design drones, operate them skillfully, and apply the latest in imaging technology is at an all-time

US military roboticists and engineers helped invent this tiny drone, known as a Close-in Covert Autonomous Disposable Aircraft, or Cicada. Its cost of $1,000 is expected to drop to as low as $250 apiece.

high. The impact of this growth will lead to an estimated one hundred thousand new jobs by 2025. Colleges and universities are introducing majors and minors to help fill the need for professionals who can step into these emerging career opportunities.

Bachelor's-degree and master's-degrees programs in areas such as professional aviation flight technology, aviation management, and unmanned aircraft space systems offer coursework that prepares students for many of the ways in which drones are used, such as hazardous operations, surveillance and data collection, secure operations, long-duration operations, highly repetitive operations, and autonomous operations. Courses covering topics such as unmanned sensing systems, UAS payload application, UAS flight simulation, UAS mission planning, robotic technologies, and computing in aerospace and aviation will enable graduates of these programs to be able to operate drones for everything from simple inspection missions to more complex missions that involve extensive planning by larger teams.

In addition, engineering degrees are also available in topics such as unmanned and autonomous systems engineering or mechanical and aerospace engineering. These degrees focus on engineering coursework designed to prepare students to enter jobs where they will design and develop drones and other unmanned aircraft. Coursework includes engineering-based courses such as strength of materials, materials science, engineering design, engineering dynamics, electronic instrumentation, thermodynamics, systems dynamics, operational applications, physics, and more.

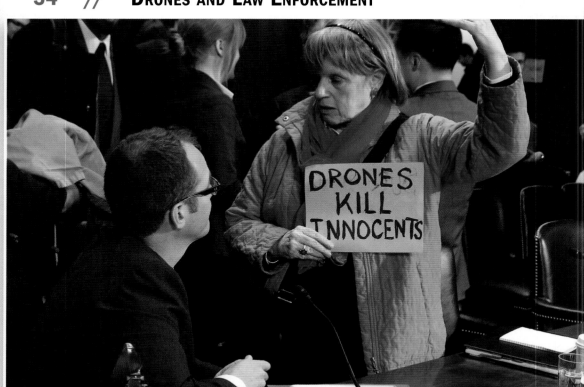

PROTESTER JOAN STALLARD (*RIGHT*), A MEMBER OF THE ANTI-WAR GROUP CODE PINK, SPEAKS WITH BENJAMIN MILLER, A DRONE SPOKESMAN FROM COLORADO, DURING A WASHINGTON, DC, HEARING.

The day may come sooner than we think when humans have become secondary in drone deployment and operation. As programming and technology become more sophisticated, law enforcement may employ ever more intuitive unmaned aerial vehicles. When it comes to the drones of the future, the sky is truly the limit.

GLOSSARY

APPREHEND To arrest or catch a criminal or fugitive.

ARSENAL A collection of weapons or a place where weapons are stored.

AUTONOMOUS Describes a thing or person that is able to control itself, or to act independently.

COMPLIANCE Following rules or regulations put in place by an official body.

CONCENTRIC Two things that have the same center; usually refers to concentric circles.

CONFISCATE To take someone else's property or belongings.

CONTRABAND Goods that are brought into the country without permission, and thus illegally, or are illegal to possess to begin with.

ELEVATION The height of something above a certain level, often sea level.

INFRACTION The breaking of a law or a rule.

INTERDICTION Delaying, disrupting, or destroying contraband, especially illegal narcotics.

METEOROLOGY The science of studying the atmosphere.

PHOTOGRAMMETRY Using photography to survey and map the distances between objects.

POACHER A person who hunts and kills wild animals illegally.

PREEMPT To take action to prevent something from happening.

PROTOTYPE A preliminary model of something that will be made or manufactured later.

RECONNAISSANCE Observation or spying to identify an enemy or enemy activities.

RECONSTRUCT To build or recreate something after it has been destroyed or damaged.

SURVEILLANCE Close observation of something.

SUSTAINABLE Maintaining something at a certain rate of production or output.

TACTICAL Characterized by planning to gain an advantage.

VIOLATION An act that is against the law or the rules.

FOR MORE INFORMATION

Airborne Law Enforcement Association
50 Carroll Creek Way, Suite 260
Frederick, MD 21701
(301) 631-2406
Website: http://alea.org
The Airborne Law Enforcement Association is a nonprofit educational
organization that supports and encourages the use of aircraft in public safety.
The organization offers educational seminars and training as well as general
information.

Association of Unmanned Vehicle Systems International (AUVSI)
2700 S. Quincy Street, Suite 400
Arlington, VA 22206
(703) 845-9671
Website: http://www.auvsi.org
AUVSI is the world's largest nonprofit organization devoted to advancing the drone,
unmanned systems, and robotics community.

Drone Pilots Association
email: peter@dronepilotsassociation.com
Website: http://dronepilotsassociation.com
The Drone Pilots Association represents the interests of commercial and
nonhobbyist drone pilots.

Federal Aviation Administration (FAA)
US Department of Transportation
800 Independence Avenue, SW
Washington, DC 20591
(866) TELL-FAA
Website: http://www.faa.gov
The Federal Aviation Administration (FAA) is the US government agency in charge
of ensuring the safety of all civil, including commercial, aviation.

Transport Canada
330 Sparks Street
Ottawa, ON K1A 0N5
Canada
(613) 993-0055
Website: https://www.tc.gc.ca/eng/civilaviation/drone-safety.html
This federal institution is responsible for overseeing and promoting Canada's trans-
portation system. Along with other forms of civil aviation, it regulates drone use.

Unmanned Aerial Vehicle Systems Association (UAVSA)
Los Angeles, California
(866) 691-7776
Website: http://www.uavsa.org/about
Founded in 2014, the Unmanned Aerial Vehicle Systems Association (UAVSA) is the
leading association serving the growing UAS/drone community.

WEBSITES

Because of the changing number of internet links, Rosen Publishing has developed
an online list of websites related to the subject of this book. This site is updated
regularly. Please use this link to access this list:

http://www.rosenlinks.com/IWD/law

FOR FURTHER READING

Ambrosio, Donovan. *Domestic Drones: Elements and Considerations for the U.S.* Hauppauge, NY: Nova Science Publishers, 2014.

Babler, Jason. *Make: Volume 44: Fun with Drones!* San Francisco, CA: Maker Media, 2015.

Baichtal, John. *Building Your Own Drones: A Beginner's Guide to Drones, UAVs, and ROVs.* Indianapolis, IN: Que Publishing, 2015.

Dougherty, Martin. *Drones: An Illustrated Guide to the Unmanned Aircraft That Are Filling Our Skies.* London, England: Amber Books, 2015.

Gerdes, Louise I. *Drones.* Farmington Hills, MI: Greenhaven Press, 2014.

Greenhaven Press editors. *Drones.* Farmington Hills, MI: Greenhaven Press, 2016.

Kallen, Stuart. *What Is the Future of Drones?* San Diego, CA: ReferencePoint Press, 2016.

Kilby, Terry, and Belinda Kilby. *Getting Started with Drones: Build and Customize Your Own Quadcopter.* San Francisco, CA: Maker Media, 2015.

Marsico, Katie. *Drones.* New York, NY: Scholastic Library Publishing, 2016.

Masters, Nancy Robinson. *Drone Pilot.* North Mankato, MN: Cherry Lake Publishing, 2013.

Norris, Donald. *Build Your Own Quadcopter.* New York, NY: McGraw-Hill Education, 2014.

Rauf, Don. *Getting the Most Out of Makerspaces to Build Unmanned Aerial Vehicles.* New York, NY: Rosen Publishing Group, 2014.

Ripley, Tim. *Military Jobs: Drone Operators.* New York, NY: Cavendish Square Publishing, 2015.

Wesselhoeft, Conrad. *Dirt Bikes, Drones, and Other Ways to Fly.* New York, NY: Houghton Mifflin Harcourt, 2015.

BIBLIOGRAPHY

Anderson, Chris. "Agricultural Drones Relatively Cheap Drones with Advanced Sensors and Imaging Capabilities Are Giving Farmers New Ways to Increase Yields and Reduce Crop Damage." *Technology Review*, Retrieved May 6, 2016 (https://www.technologyreview.com/s/526491/agricultural-drones).

Atheron, Kelsey. "How Drones Will Fight Poachers to Save Endangered Species." *Popular Science*, May 8, 2013 (http://www.popsci.com/technology/article/2013-05/what-do-drones-and-elephants-have-do-international-crime).

BBC News. "Drones: What Are They and How Do They Work?" January 31, 2012 (http://www.bbc.com/news/world-south-asia-10713898).

Blackhurst, Rob. "The Air Force Men Who Fly Drones in Afghanistan by Remote Control." *Telegraph*, September 24, 2012 (http://www.telegraph.co.uk/news/uknews/defence/9552547/The-air-force-men-who-fly-drones-in-Afghanistan-by-remote-control.html).

Bond, Michaelle. "Drones a Benefit for Law Enforcement, but Raise Concerns." Govtech.com, August 10, 2015 (http://www.govtech.com/dc/articles/Drones-a-Benefit-for-Law-Enforcement-but-Raise-Concerns.html).

Danger Room staff. "Stealthy, Tiny, Deadly, Global: The Drone Revolution's Next Phase." *Wired*, August 16, 2012 (https://www.wired.com/2012/08/next-gen-drones).

FAA.gov. "Unmanned Aircraft Systems." Retrieved May 6, 2016 (https://www.faa.gov/uas).

Ferrer, Cristina. "Back to the Future: Environmental Drones Crash into Constitutional Protections." *Vermont Journal of Environmental Law*. August 11, 2014 (http://vjel.vermontlaw.edu/back-future-environmental-drones-crash-constitutional-protections).

Francescani, Chris. "Domestic Drones Are Already Reshaping U.S. Crimefighting." Reuters.com. March 4, 2013 (http://www.reuters.com/article/us-usa-drones-lawenforcement-idUSBRE92208W20130304).

Frank, Michael. "Drone Privacy: Is Anyone In Charge?" *Consumer Reports*, February 10, 2016 (http://www.consumerreports.org/electronics/drone-privacy-is-anyone-in-charge).

Gunderson, Dan. "Drone Patrol: Unmanned Craft Find Key Role in U.S. Border Security." MPRNews.com, February 19, 2015 (http://www.mprnews.org/story/2015/02/19/predator-drone).

Koebler, Jason. "North Dakota Man Sentenced to Jail In Controversial Drone-Arrest Case." *US News and World Report*, January 15, 2014 (http://www.usnews.com

/news/articles/2014/01/15/north-dakota-man-sentenced-to-jail-in-controversial
-drone-arrest-case).

Leetaru, Kalev. "How Drones Are Changing Humanitarian Disaster Response." Forbes.
com, November 9, 2015 (http://www.forbes.com/sites/kalevleetaru/2015/11/09
/how-drones-are-changing-humanitarian-disaster-response/#7c7463e16cee).

Megerian, Chris. "Gov. Jerry Brown Approves New Limits on Paparazzi Drones." *Los
Angeles Times*, October 6, 2015 (http://www.latimes.com/local/political/la-pol
-sac-brown-drones-paparazzi-20151006-story.html).

Pierre, Thomas. "Exclusive: How Cops Saved Boy From Underground Bunker." ABC-
News.com. May 31, 2013 (http://abcnews.go.com/Politics/exclusive-cops-saved-
boy-underground-bunker/story?id=19290180).

Pullen, John Patrick. "This Is How Drones Work." *Time*, April 3, 2015 (http://time
.com/3769831/this-is-how-drones-work).

Schürer, Sonny. "Drones and Corporate Security: The Future Is Now." AASolu-
tion.com, July 28, 2014 (https://www.assolution.com/2014/07/28/drones
-and-corporate-security-the-future-is-now).

Successfulstudent.org. "15 Best Drone Training Colleges." Retrieved May 6, 2016
(http://successfulstudent.org/15-best-drone-training-colleges).

Walsh, James Igoe. "Lawfare: The Effectiveness of Drone Strikes in Counterinsurgency
and Counterterrorism Campaigns." CFR.org, September 2013 (http://www.cfr.org/
united-states/lawfare-effectiveness-drone-strikes-counterinsurgency
-counterterrorism-campaigns/p31701).

Waterman, Shaun. "Drones Over U.S. Get OK from Congress. *Washington Times*,
February 7, 2012 (http://www.washingtontimes.com/news/2012/feb/7/coming
-to-a-sky-near-you/?page=all).

Wolverton, Joe. "First Man Arrested By Aid of Drone Convicted in North Dakota."
The New American, February 1, 2014 (http://www.thenewamerican.com/
usnews/constitution/item/17534-first-man-arrested-by-aid-of-drone-convicted
-in-north-dakota).

Yates, Darren. "How Drones Work." Techradar.com, July 24, 2015 (http://www
.techradar.com/us/news/world-of-tech/how-drones-work-1300056).

INDEX

ABOUT THE AUTHOR

Laura La Bella is a freelance writer and the author of more than forty nonfiction children's books. She has profiled actress and activist Angelina Jolie in *Celebrity Activists: Angelina Jolie Goodwill Ambassador to the UN*; reported on the declining availability of the world's freshwater supply in *Not Enough to Drink: Pollution, Drought, and Tainted Water Supplies*; and has examined the food industry in *Safety and the Food Supply*. La Bella lives in Rochester, New York, with her husband and two sons.

PHOTO CREDITS